What Your Advisor *Really* Means

A brokerage firm officer explains

"You *don't* get what you pay for"

Ian Sender
Warren Buffett's Vanguard Funds

IAN Books

An IAN Books paperback

Published by
IAN Books
41 Watchung Plaza, B242
Montclair, NJ 07042

Copyright © 2017 IAN Books

Cover photo: Elisabeth Simmoneau Fort

Special sales for educational use by nonprofits.
IANBooksEditor@yahoo.com

ISBN-13: 978-1542964524

ISBN-10: 1542964520

Library of Congress Control Number: 2017933095

Dewey 332.024

1. Investments. 2. Finance, Personal.
I. Sender, Ian 1948-. II. Title.

IAN Books at Amazon.com

Wealth Without Wall Street:
Buy Direct -- Avoid the Commissions, Fees, Loads

The Insiders' Guides to Buying Discount Financial Services:
Buy Direct and Save $3,000 Every Year

Drop Your Insurance:
Buy Only What You Need

Create Financial Freedom Using Your Wealth Reserve™:
Fix your financial life

The Simple Financial Life:
How to get what you want without going into debt and living
paycheck to paycheck

Build Wealth Without Extra Money or Time:
You don't need to budget or get an extra job

Leah's Money Book:
"I want to control my own money."

The Marriage Money Book:
Start Right Together Right

Build Your Own $2,000,000 Tax-FREE Wealth Reserve™:
Self-insure Self-fund your lifestyle

Stop wasting $3,000 every year:
101
financial products **NOT** to buy and why

Wealth:
What every high school graduate needs to know in the 21st century

Contents

"You don't get what you pay for"

Recently, I heard a complaint from one of our friends at a Christmas party. He told me he was going to find a new advisor because his account had grown very little in the last 6 years. He told me his advisor only charged 0.19% and still he was not making progress with his account. He wanted to show me his statements so we decided to get together.

We met for lunch and he indeed had made only a few dollars during the last 6 years. I told him that he could have earned over 13% during that time with a simple 500 index fund. His account could have doubled from what it was 6 years ago. He looked at me as if I had pulled a gun on him. Since I am retired from the industry, I told him he should ask his new advisor about a balanced fund. My wife and I hold half of our money in one that has returned about 6.5% since 2010; 9.8% a year since 1970.

My friend George hired a new advisor and he was very impressed with all the advisor's claims and graphs. He did NOT use BrokerCheck. I suggested George ask a simple question: "What is the total cost of all the funds you propose using and what have they earned." George did not ask that question. I asked George how he answered the risk/reward attitude question on the application. He said "conservative."

Well, George, I said, your advisor has no choice but to put your money in the same investments you just left—earning little.

I explained What Your Advisor REALLY Means is that you are saying you don't want to lose money. You will never earn more than what you earned before. Government short-term bond funds charge 0.50-1.00% so if they earn 1% and your advisor takes 0.19%, you will be losing money (inflation) again. Since you did not ask about a balanced (stock/bond) fund, and you did not ask for the total cost of the advisor's work, you won't know for a year what you will actually earn.

I had suggested that George treat this transaction just like he does when he gets his car fixed. "What will you do and what will it cost me." Unfortunately, he was intimidated by his advisor's presentation and gibberish about economic trends and charts.

George is not a financial analyst so he wasted two hours. No advisor knows what will happen. If he knew he would own a hedge fund. He would NOT be a salesman.

I explained <u>What Your Advisor REALLY Means</u> is that he does not know what will happen to your money when he invests it in the funds deemed for "conservative" clients by his firm. His firm will usually make sure that George's answers to the firm's application match the goals of the funds his advisor buys for him.

I explained <u>What Your Advisor REALLY Means</u> is that you are going to pay the mutual fund owners, the firm owners and the advisor every quarter and every year no matter what happens.

I explained <u>What Your Advisor REALLY Means</u> is that you are going to get a few form 1099 tax statements every January. You will have to pay tax on the gains and dividends and interest you may not even benefit from that year. If you are having that money reinvested, you won't even receive them.

George was upset and beside himself. Why didn't his new advisor explain these things to him? Why didn't he give him other options? Why didn't the advisor ask him what he intended for this money now and later? Was the money for his wife or other heirs or grandchildren in the long-term future? Why didn't his advisor ask how much he expected his money to earn over the long term if it was for heirs?

I explained <u>What Your Advisor REALLY Means</u> is that you are telling your advisor you don't know what your money could earn because you say your risk/reward is "no chance of loss." Your advisor understands you to mean you consider this money like a bank account. You are not willing to take any loss in the short term for the chance to earn more over time.

I explained <u>What Your Advisor REALLY Means</u> is that he has profiled you as a retired senior saver. To him you are not going to question the fees that you are going to give up year after year. He sees you as a low-maintenance but low-profit client. He will not have to waste time with you. You didn't ask questions at the initial interview so you won't care what happens in the future. He knows that you buy his B.S. presentation about the future of the economy and low interest rates. You will not question whatever he says.

I explained <u>What Your Advisor REALLY Means</u> is that his choices for your money are NOT driven by him but by his firm. Your contract says that he will invest using the "suitable investment" criterion NOT what is the best deal for you. On February 3, 2017, Trump halted the new Obama Fiduciary Rule.

The Fiduciary Rule would have required product sellers to provide you with low-cost choices and limit their profit as they help people with money in retirement. Huge amounts are being transferred out of 401(k)s. Without thinking, Trump has hurt the very people he professed to stand up for against product pushers. Now they will NOT have to change. Obama's rule would have made advisors act more like accountants than used car salesmen.

As former Labor Secretary Thomas Perez said in 2016: "Today's rule ensures putting the clients first is no longer a marketing slogan," "It's now the law." Trump canceled the law.

The irony is that some sellers had already lowered fees. Vanguard, the 2nd largest money manager, has forced the for-profit firms to lower fees for some time. Most advisor/brokers would have complied in a year.

Now they can continue with high-fee products that meet the firm's revenue goals NOT ours. We could still learn to shop for the BEST product for our situation but the industry does not make finding the information easy. Products and services are NOT easy to understand. They aren't transparent.

For instance, even if you are "conservative" you will never be offered a *low*-cost long-term fund or security. Even if you demand an "index" ETF or fund, your firm will still charge you the higher expense kind and add another fee. It will be the *firm*'s BEST.

What Your Advisor REALLY Means is that it is marketed by the firm as the BEST. It is like gasoline: All 94 octane is the same but my Gulf charges $1.95. Sunoco across the street charges $2.57. My neighbor swears by Sunoco--"it is better." No facts!

Since you use a "full service" firm, you do NOT check the costs of their products. The new GOLD standard for an index is Vanguard's 500 index (large stock fund) which costs 0.05% ($5 per $10,000) and earned 10.8% since 1976. If your guy/gal charges you 1% for a 'managed' account fee plus 1% expense ratio, you are giving up 63% of your potential total accumulations. This is your sign that they would have violated the fiduciary rule. You could double your long-term money by moving it to a licensed advisor on salary at Vanguard or other low-cost firm.

I explained What Your Advisor REALLY Means is that you are charged more because you are paying for **hand holding**—someone to listen to your complaints when your account does not perform. But the advisor has little control over the markets or his/her firm. The firm owner and your advisor are in business to make money the old fashioned way—charge enormous fees for the illusion that they are "managing" your money better than you or others could.

But things are changing. Just as you might save $2,000 when you buy a car if you know the market conditions, you might save $300,000 over the 30 years you invest for, if you use low-cost retirement funds. Over time, paying 0.05% instead of 2% per year in total costs will be critical to your final accumulation because of the power of compounding. As Warren Buffett has said,

> "My wealth has come from a combination of living in America, some lucky genes, and **compound interest**."

The *Fiduciary Rule* would have helped us earn more. Vanguard can manage our money for $5 per $10,000 because it is owned by the shareholders NOT by a private corporation with its *own wealthy shareholders*. Vanguard uses the same licensed reps to help clients but pays a salary not high fees and product commissions. Check your firm's bad boys.

The Vanguard approach is the one approved by Warren Buffett and other money managers not getting rich from your money. Buffett sees the market differently than Wall Street does:

> "The stock market is a device for transferring money from the **impatient to the patient**."

Patience is important in building wealth. Most investors are not patient so most investors will not have enough later. In fact, the average investor earns only 3.79% annually (vs market returns of 11.06%) according to DALBAR's QAIB.

Mr Buffett's strategy of patience earns 19.7% compounded (earn interest on interest) over time. **He does not buy and sell**—he owns the stocks of companies for a long time.

Buffett's strategy means we must leave our money alone so it can *grow*. Once we start auto-investing in securities or mutual funds, **we do nothing**. We don't need ongoing advice. Buffett has been patient for over 40 years and has grown his initial investment of $6,000 (from paper routes) to $65 **billion**.

Warren Buffett mirrors the true fiduciary: he acts as a trusted manager of your assets, with NO conflict of interest. His actions do not involve a conflict with your goals. Your broker or advisor works for his firm's benefit NOT yours. Buffett has helped his shareholders become millionaires and billionaires. For the rest of us, he advises:

"A very low-cost index is going to beat a majority of the amateur-managed money or professionally-managed money."

John Bogle, Vanguard founder, created low-cost index funds in 1975. Buffett says if we **hold** a low-cost index fund, we will beat Wall Street's professional money managers! We invest at cost. We are given unbiased advice since Vanguard does not push products.

This is the essence of the fiduciary duty. Bogle's vision was one of a fiduciary--a steward of our "mutual" assets. He learned that most professionals can't win long term because they must *always* take their profits from *our* earnings. No salesperson knows which businesses will grow quickly unless they have insider information. So you will earn less because you pay more over time. Wall Street tells us that we need them to get rich but we give up $560 billions of our earnings every year to find out that they can NOT.

Bogle saw that an index fund beat most managers by just making par—the average. By earning average market returns of 10-12% a year we will become wealthy. See page 22. Each of our $3,000 annual investments would be worth about $30,000 over 20 years in diversified stocks like those in Vanguard stock funds.

The miracle of compounding, the real source of investing success, works only if we leave our money alone. **Simple**, but hard to do. We invest in a number of successful businesses so if one fails, we still earn 10-12% a year. We let compounding work.

Today, when we buy and hold our low-cost mutual fund investments in a special account, the earnings are tax-FREE. That means we can accumulate $1 million from our $250 a month in about 33 years. We could only do that by using a NO tax, LOW fee account. The earnings are reinvested and compounded over time.

We avoid Wall Street's fees of 1%-3% and income taxes every year FOREVER. We use a tax-FREE IRS account. Taxes and fees destroy the miracle of compounding. http://www.businessinsider.com/amazing-power-of-compound-interest-2014-7

I explained What Your Advisor REALLY Means is that he and

his firm *take fees no matter* how much we earn or lose. The firm makes money on transactions AND annual fees no matter what.

There is a better way. We invest the same amount automatically. We don't need advise to do that. If you and your spouse contribute $250 a month, each of you could have $500,000 in about <u>28</u> years. By investing a fixed amount each month, we can buy shares at the least cost possible. We buy more shares when the price is low—on sale. We buy less when the price is high--"dollar cost averaging."

With this account, we don't need to take distributions until we want to. Most pensions and IRAs require distributions and taxes at age 70.5. <u>Heirs don't have to pay taxes on this account either</u>.

Both of you invest in high-earning securities over time. We let the miracle of compounding work. We pay $168,000 in 28 years for $1,000,000. We don't stop investing when the market goes up or down. We make investing automatic. The miracle happens because we do NOTHING. We have more because we pay less! We do not trade or time the market with this money until retirement.

If you work for others, you don't have the experience of the rise and fall of a business. Most wealthy people trust CPAs not financial advisors. Wealthy people have learned that there is **no quick way** to become wealthy.

I explained <u>What Your Advisor REALLY Means</u> is that he cannot teach you the investing experience of being **patient** with your assets. Even after I show George how an account can fall and rise on page 22, he can only understand by doing.

Our friend George never had this experience so he didn't realize that we earn a huge reward for a small risk in any given year of investing. His brother had the experience of holding tight for a temporary paper "loss" and now he is a millionaire.

Buffett and Bogle made investing easier for us. The hard part is allowing our money to *work for us after we work for it*.

I explained <u>What Your Advisor REALLY Means</u> is that he is NOT going to teach you how to do NOTHING with your money.

1

Create $1,000,000 tax-FREE accounts

Building a $1 million tax-FREE account takes time. If we own a business, we learn it takes a long time—a lifetime. We would have to find and sell the right product to the right customer in a profitable manner. It is difficult to come up with a completely new product or way to sell it like Apple has done. If we are lucky, we could buyout our boss after working at a skilled trade for years. Many wealthy people have followed this path.

We must begin where we are. To build wealth is to take some of our money and buy the stocks of growing companies. We can each accumulate $500,000 over time. If we both use low-cost mutual funds in tax-FREE accounts, it will take about 28 years.

We can understand how this can happen by following the growth of a broad market index mutual fund. **Time is the key** to building wealth. Wealthy people typically invest in many types of investments, businesses and real estate. We begin with investments of $250 a month in mutual funds with many businesses.

If we are going to accumulate $1,000,000 in about 33 years, we need to find investments that can earn 10% to 12% a year, on average, over time. We must understand the reward and risk tradeoff. If we want to have a $1 million in the future, we could wait 80 years for our $500 a month to grow in a bank at 2% or wait about 26 years in a bunch of stocks of companies. We are trading time for the bank's guarantee to pay interest **every day**. We don't need that guarantee. We need the high probability that companies will profit and grow over time. That is best for the long-term.

Investing in stocks provides our best chance of success. The value of a stock market index—a bunch of stocks—has varied greatly in any one year. However, over any 10 years, the value has ALWAYS increased. This is the reason wealthy people have most of their money in the stocks of growing companies.

Remember, we are looking for investments that compound our money at 10-12% on average **over time**. The reward profile of owning a bunch of stocks is like owning a growing business—in any one year, we might have a loss or a gain. But over time we have more profits than losses and thus accumulate $1,000,000.

Bank savings are a great place to park our money for a year in case we need it to repair our car, appliances or house. However, bank savings are not really an investment. People who put their money in the bank because they think it is "safe" are not thinking about the long-term. Bank accounts are actually losing money. Inflation is eating away at the value of their savings.

Inflation is historically about 3%. If we earn 3% or less on our money, we are losing purchasing power. This means that it now costs $0.49 to mail a first class letter instead of $0.06 as it did in 1970. Sending a letter went up at about 5% a year. In order to have enough money to mail a letter in retirement, we are going to need to invest our LONG-TERM money in an investment earning more than 5%. This goes for all the money we will need to buy things in the future.

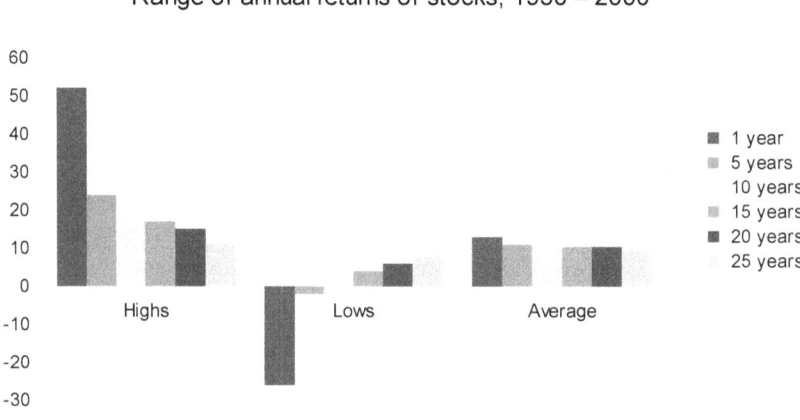

Range of annual returns of stocks, 1950 – 2000

There are few investments that we can easily buy that have the same long-term annual returns of stocks of growing companies. The graph on page 11 presents the relative growth of different types of investments and inflation. Over long-periods of time, government bonds grow at a rate a little above the rate of inflation. Large company stocks like GE and P&G grow at a higher rate and thus accumulate larger values in our account. Smaller companies grow much faster and make our account even larger over time. However, as the graph shows, the index line can be very jagged on a monthly and even yearly basis. Values do go up over time.

The graph makes it pretty clear that in order to accumulate $1,000,000 from monthly contributions, we must buy and hold the securities of growing companies worldwide, at cost, AND pay **zero** tax on the growth to maximize compounding. We can see clearly that investing in growing company stocks is more likely to get us to our goal in our lifetime than investing in government bonds or a bank savings account. Investing requires the long view.

This graph shows the accumulation over time without paying taxes each year on our earnings or annual fees to an advisor or broker. It does show that over most periods greater than 10 years, our account value grows more with stocks.

Some wealthy people also invest in gold, real estate, and alternative investment schemes. But these investments do NOT usually represent a large portion of their portfolio. These investments do not come without significant costs and significant risk. They do NOT show the same consistent long-term growth pattern that growing global companies do.

According to a number of studies, gold, real estate and other investments have annual average returns under 10%. When we subtract the costs of buying, maintaining and securing these investments, we give up a lot of the gains. We can use an online compounding calculator to become familiar with total accumulations at different rates of return—3, 5, 7, 9, 11, etc. http://www.moneychimp.com/calculator/compound_interest_calcul ator.htm

For instance, if an investment requires taxes to be paid each year, this cancels some of the compounding effect on the total accumulation over time. Since we wish to reach $1 million as soon as possible, we must use a tax-advantaged account to hold our low-cost investments. Depending on our tax bracket (taxable income) we may reduce our total accumulation by over half because we lose the compounding effect. The chart below gives us an idea of what can happen in 30 years. Most retirement accounts are tax-DEFERRED; not tax-FREE. Taxes have to be paid sometime.

As you have probably guessed, the wealthy have already figured out how to pay less tax on their wealth. The American tax system taxes <u>earned</u> income at higher rates than <u>investment</u> income. Plus we must pay federal and state income taxes, excise taxes, Social Security and Medicare taxes, perhaps unemployment and disability income taxes as well as sales tax on most goods.

For the wealthy, like Warren Buffett, with $65 billions of assets, most of his income is from his company stock gains and dividends. He admitted, "I pay at a lower overall tax rate than all of my office employees." He pays only 17% **total** tax. Listen and weep: http://www.youtube.com/watch?v=Cu5B-2LoC4s.

We are not at that stage yet. Most of us have income which is taxed as earned income and goes straight to the government before we have a chance to pay less tax. Even self-employed people must pay taxes as they go—at least once a quarter. Only the wealthy and large companies can afford most tax avoidance schemes. Fortunately, Congress created one for working people. The Roth IRA lets us avoid income tax on the earnings altogether.

Tax-FREE v Taxable

In order for us to become wealthy we must find a way to avoid paying tax on our $1,000,000 account as it accumulates. Traditional pensions, 401k and IRAs just delay taxes—taxes must be paid later as the money comes out of the account AND at higher earned income tax rates. Thus even when our investment money is growing it is converted to earned income money for tax purposes. Unlike Mr Buffett, we NEVER get to pay the wealthy people (capital gains) rate of 15-20%.

Luckily, there is now a solution for us to match the tax advantage that the wealthy have. In fact, only we can use it. We use the Roth IRA, a tax-FREE IRS trust, to compound the high returns of the stocks of growing companies over time. We avoid the greatest killer of wealth—taxes—and let time transform our $168,000 in contributions into $1 million. Patience and simple buy and hold investing in a tax-FREE account make our strategy beat the industry myth of genius (expensive) stock pickers.

The hard part of investing is leaving our money alone to grow like the Biblical mustard seed into a mustard tree.

Various investment accumulations

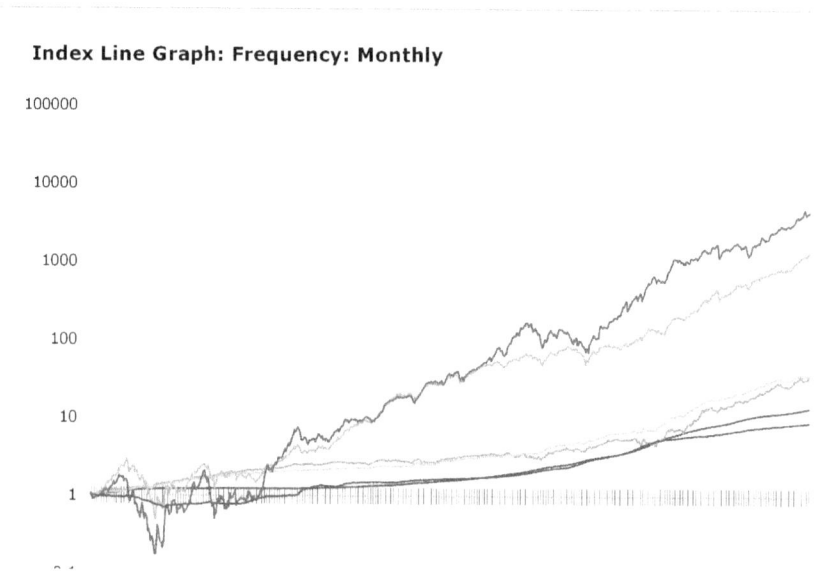

Top line—Small Cap Stocks
2nd line—Large Cap Stocks (S&P 500)
3rd line—US Long-term Corporate Bonds
4th line—Intermediate-term Government Bonds
5th line—US 30 day Government T-bills
6th line—US inflation

Courtesy: Dr. Campbell R. Harvey http://www.duke.edu/~charvey/

2

Use a tax-favored lifetime investment account

The solution to our retirement problem came in 1997. Senator Roth created the Roth IRA. This tax-FREE account provides the protection we need to allow our contributions to compound without taxation every year AND later when we take the gains out. We never have to pay taxes on the earnings, dividends and interest we earned on our money. We don't even pay the tax-advantaged capital gains rate of the wealthy!

Ben Franklin was wrong! Only death is certain, not taxes. The only thing we give up with this account is an immediate tax deduction. However, compare the value of paying a little more tax (15%-25% on $3,000) now with paying ZERO tax later. We can spend $40,000 tax-FREE for every $3,000 a year we contributed over time. We can see the fantastic advantage we now have. This is a better deal than most wealthy people have.

Tax-FREE accumulation and tax-FREE income after age 59 1/2 is a huge bonus. It is like receiving $300,000 FREE on our $1 million account. Also, because we already paid tax on the contributions, we pay no tax if we take contributions out for emergencies. This can make a big impact on our borrowing costs when we take money out to buy an appliance, a car repair, a down payment or temporary living expenses.

Using this account, both our total contributions of $168,000 over time grow to over $1,000,000 and we don't have to pay any federal or state income tax on the earnings. WOW! Since we pay no tax, Uncle Sam is really helping us out in meeting our goals. All we have to do is use this special IRS tax haven and keep making contributions. We **Keep More of What We Earn**.

This special account is the IRS §408 trust. We have to follow the rules to gain this amazing tax advantage but the Roth IRA rules are pretty simple—taxed money goes in and tax-FREE earnings come out after age 59 ½. We can take our contributions out anytime.

Why is this account special? Every other type of investment account requires that taxes be paid now or later. Mutual funds declare gains each year just like a bank CD and we need to pay tax. Our retirement accounts and annuities are tax-deferred. We pay tax when we take money out. Even life insurance with cash value requires taxes to be paid unless it is a death benefit to heirs. Even assets like individual stocks or ETFs or our own company equity held for long term gains will require taxes eventually when sold. The gains in this account are FREE—no tax ever.

Contributions are limited to $5,500 (2014), but may rise in future years. http://www.irs.gov/publications/p590/ch02.html There are income limits of $129,000 (2014) or $191,000 married. We make our deposit to our Roth IRA **account** automatic so we can't forget to do it each month.

We may also invest in our employer's Roth 401k if it is offered. The contributions grow tax FREE forever. We can contribute more to this account. We will have tax-FREE income from the account later. Contributions to a regular 401k can be converted later. We can limit taxes by converting small portions of our 401k or regular IRA each year.

We can make contributions to our Roth 401k only if our employer offers it in the retirement plan. We may prefer to be taxed before our retirement since tax rates are bound to be higher later and our balances are smaller at the beginning.

There are no limits on an employee's income in determining if he or she can make designated Roth 401(k) contributions. If we decide to invest $6,000 a year for about 26 years in a low-cost stock fund inside our employer's Roth 401k plan, we could accumulate $1 million with NO income taxation to pay on the earnings. The tax savings might be worth an extra 30% since our federal and state tax payments are avoided. We **Keep More of What We Earn**.

The catch: If we take the *earnings* out before age 59.5, we must pay income tax, unless we use $10,000 for our first home, are disabled, or die. The account must be open at least 5 years to take money out. However, if we take out *contributions*, we pay no tax. If we pay our 'loan' back to our own account, we can still reach our goal. The hard part is leaving our money alone to grow tax-FREE.

Let's say we need $15,000 to buy a luxury used car. As we can see from the chart on page 22, taking $15,000 from an account worth $250,000 is very different from taking $15,000 from one worth only $45,000. Both are contributions and are not taxable but borrowing 40% of the account this early stunts its growth.

A patient millionaire finds a way to save the $15,000 separately or keep driving the old car. The power of compounding is too valuable to lose by raiding the account too early. One story about billionaire Buffett will illustrate the habits of the wealthy. Mr Buffett is said to have driven (no chauffeur) his VW Beetle long after he became a multimillionaire. Buffett did not like to lose money and a new car loses 40% of its value quickly. He thought that the $40,000-new-car cost, invested at 10%, is worth about $80,000 in 10 years. So he kept driving the old VW.

Monthly	Accumulation at 12% per year									
	5	10	15	20	25	30	35	40	45	50
$100	$8,167	$23,004	$49,958	$98,925	$187,884	$349,496	$643,095	$1,176,477	$2,145,469	$3,905,834
$200	$16,334	$46,008	$99,916	$197,850	$375,768	$698,992	$1,286,190	$2,352,954	$4,290,938	$7,811,668
$300	$24,501	$69,012	$149,874	$296,775	$563,652	$1,048,488	$1,929,285	$3,529,431	$6,436,408	$11,717,502
$500	$40,835	$115,020	$249,790	$494,625	$939,420	$1,747,480	$3,215,475	$5,882,385	$10,727,346	$19,529,169

Most clients are not that thrifty. They use their contributions to buy a used car to avoid new car depreciation and new appliances, vacations, and other necessities AFTER they have a sizable account. When both family wage earners contribute to their Roth IRAs, they can easily reach a quarter of a million dollars in 15 years. That means $90,000 are contributions and then some of it can be used to pay cash instead of buying on credit.

Wealthy people use their wealth to pay cash. They never PAY interest. Paying interest on a debt is the reverse of compounding. Someone else is becoming wealthy from us. The wealthy always EARN interest. They use the chart above or the http://www.moneychimp.com/calculator/compound_interest_calcul ator.htm to determine what the real cost of buying something on credit will be just like Buffett did. Why give up $80,000 when we can drive the old car a little longer. Buffett could have bought 100 new cars and it wouldn't have changed his wealth or lifestyle, but he didn't. His habit is to live frugally and not look wealthy.

We can use this account (its contributions) to cover our liability insurance deductibles also. We can save thousands of dollars by using the highest deductibles on our car, home and health insurance. Self-insurance is also the way to avoid any changes in our policy costs. Insurers are less likely to drop us if we don't make claims for small amounts. If we take care of our out-of-pocket medical expenses, we may find a low-cost comprehensive policy if we need to buy health coverage.

The rules for the use of our Roth IRA account are manageable by ourselves. We don't need an advisor. They are found at irs.gov/retirement/article/0,,id=137307,00.html. Our account trustee can answer most questions. We don't need to pay an attorney. All of the large low-cost mutual funds firms are trustees. We will discuss the best firms available below.

We can start this account with any of the firms with no upfront charges. Most do charge an annual fee for the investments and an annual bookkeeping fee. We will consider the specific investment options later. We will use low-cost firms only. We will keep more.

It is important to pick a trustee with the least costs since over time the annual costs can really destroy our accumulations. For instance, if we use a brokerage firm as trustee, we might have to pay 2% or more each year on the balance. The difference is huge. If both spouses have a low-cost account with contributions of $250 a month for about 26 years, they could accumulate $1,000,000. If they use a high-cost broker/advisor, both accounts may hit only $500,000. Depending on earnings of 8-10% using a broker/advisor (fees of 2-3% per year), they could really hurt themselves. We need to watch the costs. We compare the benefits of firms below.

We can open our account at any age as long as we have *earned* income—stock dividends or interest do not count. Any job will do. We don't even need a job requiring a W-2 to prove it. A part-time, weekend or night job will do. Any cash-only work will also qualify. Accountants recommend that receipts and records be maintained. We could even work for ourselves in a home-office business. This also provides a tax advantage in retirement.

Nontaxable distributions from a Roth IRA won't affect our eligibility for a child's student aid. Later, in retirement, this money won't raise the taxes on our Social Security benefits.

We can make contributions to both our individual Roth IRA and our Roth account at work (401k). The limits change each year, so check Pub 590: http://www.irs.gov/pub/irs-pdf/p590.pdf.

Avoiding taxes on the annual gains of our accumulations is one of the few Congressional tax havens for working people. This special account is the IRS §408 trust. We have to follow the rules of a Roth IRA to gain this amazing tax advantage. The rules are pretty simple: pay smaller tax on contributions now in exchange for NO tax on huge gains later—over time, the $832,000 earnings ($1 million minus $168,000) are tax-FREE. We can use the contributions to avoid paying interest to banks for our major purchases. *We earn interest, we don't pay interest*. This account is the perfect tax shelter for working people. And it is simple to set up and run each year. In the future, we can spend $30,000 tax-FREE for every $3,000 we invest each year.

Tax-FREE v Taxable

Actual client, Tom's account, investing $3,000 per year, 1962-2003

24%	3,720
16%	7,795
12%	12,091
-10%	13,582
24%	20,561
11%	26,153
-8%	26,821
4%	31,013
14%	38,775
19%	49,713
-14%	45,333
-26%	35,766
37%	53,110
24%	69,576
-8%	66,770
6%	73,956
18%	90,809
32%	123,827
-5%	120,486
22%	150,653
21%	185,920
6%	200,255
32%	268,297
19%	322,843
5%	342,135
17%	403,808
32%	536,987
-3%	523,787
31%	690,091
8%	748,538
10%	826,692
2%	846,286
38%	1,172,015
23%	1,445,268
33%	1,926,197
28%	2,469,372
21%	2,991,570
-9%	2,725,059
-12%	2,403,420
-22%	1,874,601
29%	2,412,905

3

Compound high earnings over time

2016 Total Return	Fund	Long-term Return	Longevity
11.9%	500 Index	10.9%*	since 1976
33.1%	Energy	10.9%	since 1984
16.1%	Extended Market	10.7%	since 1987
-9.0%	Health	16.4%	since 1984
1.7%	International Growth	10.0%	since 1981
10.7%	PRIMECAP	13.4%	since 1984
18.3%	Small Cap Index	10.7%	since 1960
8.1%	Wellesley Income	9.9%	since 1970
12.5%	Windsor	11.3%	since 1958
13.4%	Windsor II	10.7%	since 1985
11.7%	Average	11.5%	

*Average Annual Returns as of 12/31/16.

The wealthy earn 10% to 12% on their money. We could buy all ten Vanguard funds and receive 11.5% total return with less risk than owning just one fund. When one fund is down, others are up.

Compounding the earnings is key. The rich get richer—the top 1% take 23.5% of all income (up from 8.9%). And, as many millionaires have said, "the first million is the hardest." If we start with $6,000, it will take us about 20 years of investing $6,000 a year in stock funds to reach $500,000 (and only in a tax-FREE low-fee account).

However, when we reach a **1/2** million dollars, we only have to double our money to reach $1 million. Investors in stock mutual funds, earning 10-12% on average, do this in about 8 years without adding new money. Our low-fee tax-FREE account makes it easier to reach our goal. We pay no advisor costs because we use a simple strategy and let the markets do what they do.

Compounding of high earnings means that we make money on our last period's accumulations. The progression looks like the client's account values on the previous page. Notice that our balance can double in a few good years. This happens because we are not just adding money each month, but adding up to 38% of the previous year's accumulation to our balance. We are making money on top of our money with no extra effort on our part. During this 40 year period, this client 'lost' money some years. In fact, he lost 14% and then 26% back to back, but then made 37% and 24%.

Wealthy people don't panic. They have learned that compounding over the long term is the only way they can build wealth. There are no successful get-rich-quick schemes. To reach their goal, they know there will be setbacks. No business grows steadily upward all the time. They have seen the losses before and they don't sell their assets in a panic. They remain **patient**.

We will buy assets that "grow by themselves." We will have security because our ***purchasing power*** will grow over time. If we doubt that the wealthy invest in the stock market for security, take a look at the long-term returns for various Vanguard mutual funds where they put their money. These funds have provided investors with $1,000,000 or more for their retirement. During the recent recession, Vanguard had inflows not outflows.

2015 Total Return	Fund	Long-term Return	Longevity
1.4%	500 Index	10.8%*	since 1976
-21.5%	Energy	10.3%	since 1984
-3.3%	Extended Market Idx	10.6%	since 1987
12.7%	Health	17.3%	since 1984
-0.7%	International Growth	10.3%	since 1981
2.6%	PRIMECAP	13.5%	since 1984
-3.6%	Small Cap Index	10.5%	since 1960
1.3%	Wellesley Income	9.9%	since 1970
-3.3%	Windsor	11.3%	since 1958
-3.2%	Windsor II	10.6%	since 1985
-1.7%	Average	11.5%	

*Average Annual Returns as of 12/31/15.

This kind of security comes from our simple strategy—automatic contributions … and patience. The miracle of compounding works its magic on our money when we give it TIME. The wealthy give their money time to compound. They don't take it out. They try not to pay tax every year on the gains. They maintain their contribution schedule because each $100 added is worth $10,000 to them later. They use the compound interest calculator so they know the future value: moneychimp.com/calculator/compound_interest_calculator.htm.

Compounding of high earnings requires patience but has a big bang. Most people who become wealthy have to put up with years of waiting. At the beginning of the accumulation, especially if we have a loss or two, we may get discouraged and quit. The account just doesn't seem to adding up to an inspiring total.

It took this client 21 years to get to $150,000. Then it only took 14 years to get to a $1,172,015. After only 4 years, it became $3,000,000. Shortly thereafter he "lost" over a million dollars!

This client stuck with it and was successful in reaching the goal but there are many who did not. Most people who are not wealthy already, have a hard time believing it can happen with their *patience*. They just don't have the experience of how compounding works to keep faith in its outcome eventually.

If you already have a Roth IRA with significant values, you can use it to do your gift and estate planning. You don't have to take the money out beginning at age 70½, unlike the regular IRA or pension. You can let it grow. You can name your family members as beneficiaries which will extend the miracle of compounding. Obviously, as beneficiary, your grandchild could just liquidate the account and thus lose the value of their "Gift of a Lifetime." Wealthy people use a knowledgable attorney to make sure their wealth passes to those who will make the most of it.

Once an account becomes sizable, we don't need to add contributions to it. Usually, by the time we stop regular employment, we aren't making contributions. This account cannot accept contributions unless they are the result of earned income. Some wealthy people continue to work after age 65 because they love what they do and want to continue. Obviously, they don't need to work. The miracle of compounding continues.

One of the best examples of the potential of growth by compounding is seen in the accumulation of investor Anne Scheiber. With below average wages, this woman invested in quality companies which paid dividends and gains. There were no Roth IRAs. She reinvested her dividends and gains and at her death gave $22 million to Yeshiva University for a scholarship designed to help support women.

Getting "the first half million is the hardest."

The annual returns of growing companies

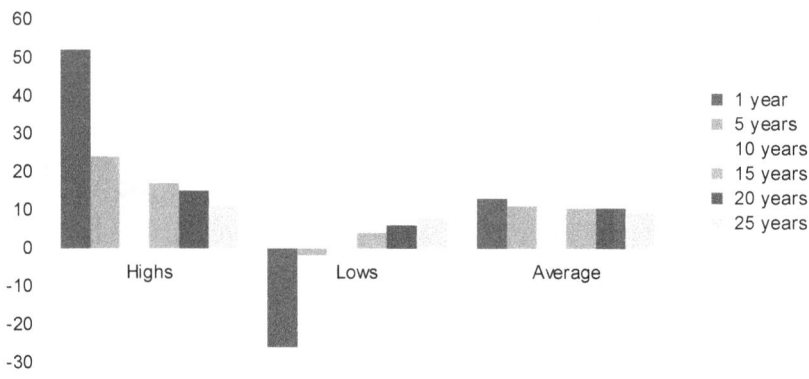

Range of annual returns of stocks, 1950 – 2000

Legend:
- 1 year
- 5 years
- 10 years
- 15 years
- 20 years
- 25 years

Categories: Highs, Lows, Average

4

Set up automatic monthly contributions early

The Value of Starting Early

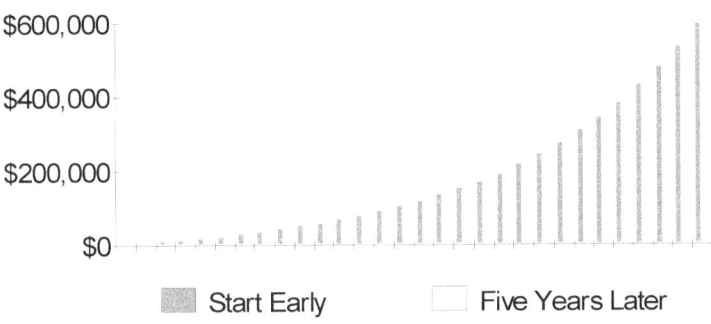

Our simple strategy for building wealth requires consistent additions to our accounts. Making it automatic helps take our emotions out of the process. We gain true power. We do not panic like others. We do not watch the market or our account. If we don't have to write and send the contribution check each month, we won't think about how our account is doing.

Our normal reaction to having money in an account is to watch it, guard it, think about how it is doing, compare its size and rate of growth. We pay advisors to watch too. All of these actions are fine for a savings account. But as a silent partner in growing companies, this is not wise. We have to believe that global businesses will continue to grow. However, most people don't look at their wealth-building in that way. Most people do not think of their accounts as a stake in many growing businesses.

One way we can help change our thinking is to try to put the account out of our immediate concern by making the contributions automatic. Like the Social Security contributions we make every payday, the contributions are made automatically. This can happen easily with a Roth 401k since our Plan administrator will deduct the amount we specify at Plan enrollment. In the same manner, we can have the Roth IRA trustee debit our checking account automatically every month.

As one client told me, "I never see the deduction, so I never miss it." Of course this client had already identified the $250 he had committed to his $2,000,000 future years ago. He says that he would just waste the $250 on a car lease anyway. He had been doing that for years because he never took the trouble to set his goals for short-term and long-term timelines. He went through his spending with a knife. He used our Guides to find the $250 a month he was wasting on products and services he would never use or need. In my amazon.com/Insiders-Guides-Discount-Financial-Services/ you will find "tricks of the trade" that we insiders use to buy directly from quality manufacturers.

Many people have trouble keeping up the habit of investing every month. Some emergency always interupts this process. The delay in the periodic contributions causes the compounding effect to be reduced. The interruption is like starting the investment process late. This chart shows us what starting early or not putting off the investments can do. Over time, the delay compounds the lack of accumulation. Starting 5 years later means ending up with HALF the amount we were shooting for. It is hard to believe that missing that $250 a month for 5 years or $15,000 can reduce our total from $600,000 to $300,000. It's easy to say **I will start later**.

This is why our contributions to the account should not pass through our hands. We should have the money taken directly from our bank account by the trustee. Contributions are after-tax so you can take them from your future, when necessary. Nontaxable distributions from a Roth IRA won't affect your eligibility for student aid either. Later, in retirement, this money won't affect your Social Security benefits, which are subject to taxation depending on your income. Even muni bond income is counted in the tax worksheet for Social Security benefits. irs.gov/pub/irs-pdf/p915.pdf

The second reason why this technique for developing wealth works is that when contributions are automatic, we do not have the temptation to try to time the market. Many people want to know the secret to timing the market so that they can invest right at the bottom of market cycles and sell at the peak of the market.

Unfortunately, it is a myth that we can do this consistently.

Again, this is our misconception of how building wealth works. Yes, there are lucky gamblers. However, they are the exception. We use compounding. We want to end up with $1,000,000 tax-FREE. We are silent partners in building businesses that produce dividends and gains over time. We are NOT placing our contributions on the red or black at the casino.

Our account grows with steady contributions because in the month we buy shares in a mutual fund, we receive less shares when the price is high and more shares when the price is low. Studies have shown that this is better than investing our $3,000/$6,000 all at once. It is not possible to know when the shares we buy will be at their lowest cost in the year going forward. Again, over time, we will own more shares at the least cost because we are buying more when the price is low.

This can be illustrated by considering how hard it is to find the lowest price at any given time in the market. There were ONLY 40 days from 1950 to 2007 that produced 70% of all the S&P 500 index's total returns. That is 40 out of 14,528. We can't possibly know when to buy into the businesses represented in the mutual fund we are using. We will lose money if we become traders who try to time the market well. Traders lose money most of the time. See John Bogle's analysis in *Don't Count on It*, p 169.

The key to wealth is patience: let compounding work. Over time, stocks of growing companies have the most consistent record of providing 10%-12% annual returns. We just don't know which companies and which time to invest are best. Luckily, we don't have to know. We just need to understand compounding tax-FREE.

The bigger picture is that we want our account accumulation to grow exponentially. We want to take advantage of the miracle of compounding. Since we don't have wealth now, we are going to have to be patient to acquire it. We want every dollar we invest to count. We have $250/$500 a month to invest so we have to rely on consistent buying of shares to reach our goal.

Accumulations double in value every 8-10 years if they are concentrated in the top two lines below. Of course the stock market doesn't move up at 10-12% EACH year. However, our account will double and double and double so that in about 26 years, we could have $1/2 million each. Notice how the account values in the chart on page 22 for this client double—from $1 million to $2 million in 8 years, even with 3 years of losses. Of course, a million dollars will be worth less in the future because of inflation. But we will certainly appreciate our account values later no matter what our contributions are now. Consistency over time builds wealth.

Cumulative Wealth

Index Line Graph: Frequency: Monthly

Top line—Small Cap Stocks
2nd line—Large Cap Stocks (S&P 500)
3rd line—US Long-term Corporate Bonds
4th line—Intermediate-term Government Bonds
5th line—US 30 day Government T-bills
6th line—US inflation

Courtesy: Dr. Campbell R. Harvey http://www.duke.edu/~charvey/

And the bonus of this geometric account growth is that it does not quit even after we stop adding our monthly contributions. Once the account has reached a certain mass, let's say after 20 years of $6K contributions or $120,000, it will keep compounding. On page 32 we show you how this worked for contributions of $2,000 to a virtual account invested in the U.S. stock market (top 500 firms) over time.

We see in the chart "**Cumulative Wealth**" above that wealth accumulates at different rates depending on the type of assets we buy. For anyone who invested in smaller companies over any given

15 year period, the benefits were outstanding. For each $1,000 invested in 1940, $3,000,000 was the total return by the 1990's. Investing more cautiously in the large companies of the S&P 500, for instance, our $1,000 would have grown to almost a $1,000,00 by 2000. Yes, the lines are not perfectly straight, but growing $500 a month to $1,000,000 is definitely worth the ups and downs. Inflation is designated by the bottom line here. Putting all our money in the bank for 'safety' would accumulate at a rate represented by a line near that bottom line.

Of course, these different rates of wealth accumulation assume two important factors—NO taxes and LOW costs. We have eliminated the first killer of wealth—TAXES—by using a tax-FREE trust account. Costs of the investment type we use can also kill our total accumulations. The whole financial industry is built on the extraction of these costs from our accounts. We must use low-cost stock funds to have a *Tax-FREE Retirement*.

One of the most difficult parts of this strategy is sticking with the program. If we put our monthly contributions on automatic, we will have no interruptions. If we instruct our trustee to debit our savings or checking account every month, we have a high probability of meeting our goals over time. We set it and forget it. See how Earl Crawley, parking attendant, did it: http://www.youtube.com/watch?v=XD0svDGyLWU

Do Nothing.

Once we set up automatic investing, we forget we are investing in our future and thus we actually create it.

What an irony!

$2,000 Annual Stock Market Investment 1950- '70- '80- '90- 2013

Year	Returns	Balance	Balance	Balance	Balance
		$2,000			
1950	31%	$2,620			
1951	24%	$5,729			
1952	18%	$9,120			
1953	-1%	$11,009			
1954	52%	$19,773			
1955	31%	$28,523			
1956	5%	$32,049			
1957	-11%	$30,304			
1958	43%	$46,194			
1959	12%	$53,978			
1960	1%	$56,538			
1961	26%	$73,757			
1962	-8%	$69,697			
1963	24%	$88,904			
1964	16%	$105,449			
1965	12%	$120,342			
1966	-10%	$110,108			
1967	24%	$139,014			
1968	11%	$156,526			
1969	-8%	$145,844	2,000		
1970	4%	$153,757	2,080		
1971	14%	$177,563	4,651		
1972	19%	$213,681	7,915		
1973	-14%	$185,485	8,527		
1974	-26%	$138,739	7,790		
1975	37%	$192,813	13,412		
1976	24%	$241,568	19,111		
1977	-8%	$224,082	19,422		
1978	6%	$239,647	22,707		
1979	18%	$285,144	29,155	2,000	
1980	32%	$379,030	41,124	2,640	
1981	-5%	$361,978	40,968	4,408	
1982	22%	$444,053	52,421	7,818	
1983	21%	$539,724	65,850	11,879	
1984	6%	$574,228	71,921	14,712	
1985	32%	$760,621	97,575	22,060	
1986	19%	$907,519	118,494	28,632	
1987	5%	$954,995	126,519	32,163	
1988	17%	$1,119,684	150,367	39,971	
1989	32%	$1,480,623	201,125	55,402	2,000
1990	-3%	$1,438,144	197,031	55,680	1,940
1991	31%	$1,886,589	260,731	75,560	5,161
1992	8%	$2,039,676	283,749	83,765	7,734
1993	10%	$2,245,843	314,324	94,342	10,708
1994	2%	$2,292,800	322,651	98,268	12,962
1995	38%	$3,166,824	448,018	138,370	20,647
1996	23%	$3,897,654	553,522	172,656	27,856
1997	33%	$5,186,540	738,844	232,292	39,709
1998	28%	$6,641,331	948,281	299,894	53,387
1999	21%	$8,038,430	1,149,839	365,291	67,019
2000	-9%	$7,316,791	1,048,174	334,235	62,807
2001	-12%	$6,447,855	925,203	296,223	57,095
2002	-22%	$5,024,437	722,291	232,316	46,035
2003	29%	$6,459,474	930,787	301,119	61,730
2004	11%	$7,164,483	1,034,274	336,099	70,664
2005	5%	$7,512,677	1,084,540	352,433	74,098
2006	15%	$8,694,884	1,259,259	412,409	90,450
2007	5%	$9,163,538	1,327,133	434,638	95,325
2008	-39%	$5,601,431	813,388	268,074	60,754
2009	27%	$7,116,358	952,155	342,993	79,699
2010	15%	$8,186,112	1,097,278	396,742	93,954
2011	2%	$8,347,378	1,118,894	404,558	95,805
2012	16%	$9,666,264	1,295,679	468,478	110,942
2013	32%	$12,759,468	1,710,296	618,390	146,443
Avg.	12%	12%	11%	13%	11%

Ibbotson Associates **Stocks average 11.4% per year, bonds 5%, CDs 3%.** Stocks have gone up as much as 54% and as low as –43% in 1 year, up to 28% or down to –12% in 5 years, up 20% or down 0% in 10 years, up 18% or up 3% in 20 years. Short term bonds have gone up 14% or up 0% in 1 year, up 11% or up 0% in 5 years, up 9% or up 0% in 10 years, up 10% or up 1% in 20 years. Check: returns: http://www.moneychimp.com/features/market_cagr.htm

5

Use low-cost mutual funds only

Cost Matters: 0.19% v 1.68%

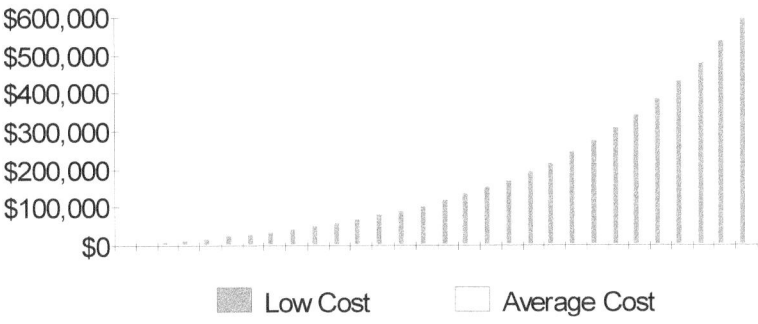

"In every single time period and data point tested,
***low-cost* funds beat high-cost funds."**

"Cost matters," fiduciary John Bogle

Wall Street claims that you must pay more for good returns. Some pay a lot to those who predict. But fund-rating analysts at Morningstar proved that Wall Street is wrong. ***Low-cost*** funds always beat high-cost funds. Predictors are paid to make educated guesses. No one can predict the future.

The **best predictor** of our wealth-building success is COST. It is common sense that there are just too many variables in the success of growing companies' stocks for anyone to be able to pick them in advance, consistently. A low-cost mutual fund provides the best chance of maximizing our accumulations as the market leaders change over time.

Contrary to Wall Street's BS, it does not matter which stocks are rising or falling at any given time. If our account holds a broad representation of stocks and our investment costs are low, we will benefit over the long haul. We own them all!

Since the annual returns of stock funds have averaged 10-12% over time, we want to pick the lowest cost mutual fund available. A stock fund that reflects an overall market is called an index fund. This kind of fund, explained below, costs only 0.07% ($7 per $10,000). Our account will compound at or near the 10-12% over time since ours costs 30-40 times less than Wall Street's. If we use the high-cost stock funds, we will earn only 6-8% over time. These funds pay managers high salaries with expensive bonuses. The fund owners and sales staff are paid well also. These funds are the cash cow of Wall Street.

The chart above makes it clear. Over time, the costs we pay each year will cut our total accumulation by a THIRD or more. Instead of compounding at 10-12% annually on average, some people give up 1-3% of the earnings on their money to the middle person. They end up with less. They subsidize Wall Street.

John Bogle, founder of the largest mutual fund firm, estimates that working people give up 63% of their total accumulations.

Wall Street says that we can earn more by paying a 'star' manager to pick the right stocks on an ongoing basis. The money "experts" say we get what we pay for and a proven stock-picking manager will overcome the extra costs and make more for us.

The reality is that this **myth has been proven wrong**. The lowest cost funds don't pay a star manager and owner big bucks but come out ahead over time. There are simply too many variables for anyone or computer program to pick the winning stocks all the time. Some of the lowest cost funds are called index funds. When we buy an market index, we are buying a piece of many companies. This gives us the same annual returns as the overall market over time. We pay tiny expenses. *We keep more*!

Many studies have proven that index funds beat funds run by stock pickers most of the time. Low-cost index funds beat 86% of funds with a stock-picking manager. *BusinessWeek* Apr 2009. http://www.businessweek.com/investing/insights/blog/archives/2009/04/where_have_all.html.

When we investigate the experiences of the best fiduciary money managers in the world, we find they recommend index funds to most people who invest as silent partners. Here are their statements:

Warren Buffett is probably history's greatest investor, in terms of results with $65 BILLION ($65 thousand million dollars) so far. He buys **companies** that provide valuable services to a great number of people. His company owns parts of Coke, GEICO, Fruit of the Loom, Benjamin Moore, Acme Bricks, Burlington Northern, etc. berkshirehathaway.com/

He told Reuters: "A very low-cost index is going to beat a majority of the amateur-managed money or professionally-managed money."

Compare the odds of selecting the correct mutual fund. A fund's chance of beating the market in EACH year is 3 out of 100. nytimes.com/2009/02/22/your-money/stocks-and-bonds/22stra.html

Peter Lynch, brilliant manager, Magellan Fund "…you'd be just as well off if you'd invested in the S&P 500." *One Up on Wall Street*, 1989, p. 240.

Jonathan Clements, formerly **The Wall Street Journal**
"Most people can do it themselves. ... By indexing, you don't just ensure that you will do better than most other investors. You will also enjoy the advantage of 'relative certainty.' . . . For most investors, Vanguard will be the place to go." *You've Lost It, Now What? How to beat the bear market and still retire on time*, 2003, p. 62, 70.

Charles D. Ellis, money managers' consultant
"The premise . . . that professional investment managers **can** beat the market . . . appears to be false. It is a loser's game. … clients would have done better in a market fund." Returns are "splendidly predictable—on average and over time." *Investment Policy, How to Win the Loser's Game*, 1985, p. 5, 20, 34.

Jane Bryant Quinn, consumer advisor
"I'm a longtime booster of index mutual funds. These funds follow the market as a whole. Tons of research has shown that most money managers don't beat the markets they invest in, after costs. Maybe your own stocks or funds have excelled in the past couple of years. But in most cases, you've also been taking extra risk. The

odds of superior performance are against you, in the long run. Indexing puts the odds on your side." *Los Angeles Business Journal*, May 8, 2000

Charles Schwab founder, discount broker
"I put my money where my mouth is: most of the mutual fund investments I have are in index funds, approximately 75%. My core investments are index funds. Experienced investors have discovered that in any given year, on average, only 20 to 30 percent of mutual funds outperform the market. That is why I recommend index funds…"
Mr. Schwab tells of one of his friends who owned many well-run funds. After keeping track of all the dividends, taxes, reinvestments tax basis and statements, he found he earned the same return as the index of these funds. After selling them all, he bought the index fund. He has "what he wanted in the first place: diversification, tax advantages, one statement, and lower expenses." *Guide to Financial Independence*, 1998, pp. 90, 103, 111.

Motley Fool, Internet site about investing
"Almost **everything** that you will ever read about mutual funds beyond, "Buy an index fund." is superfluous to your long-term success in investing in mutual funds." Fool.com.

Walter Updegrave, formerly senior editor, *Money*
"Mutual fund picking would be easier if there was one you could count on to outperform 70% or so of its competitors over long stretches of a decade or more. It's called an index fund. Although less than 10% of investors own an index fund, they are "one of the best-kept secrets" on Wall Street. My unabashed aim is to convince you to put at least a part of your money into one or more of these funds. You have a far less than a 50% chance of beating the market…. I strongly recommend that you make index funds your primary holding…." *The Right Way to Invest in Mutual Funds*, 1996, p 189-194.

Andrew Tobias, financial writer
"Scrimp and save, putting whatever you can into no-load, low-expense stock market index funds, both U.S. and foreign. You will do better than 80% of your friends and neighbors." *My Vast*

Fortune, 1997, p. 158.

There are many books written on the subject of index and "managed" funds. If you wish to vanquish the hype and understand investing, skim *A Random Walk Down Wall Street* by Princeton University's Burton Malkiel. Here are the reasons why smart insiders use low-cost funds:

1. Both stock and bond index funds provide better returns than 86% of managed funds for periods greater than 10 years.
2. You earn more because you pay lower costs and taxes.
3. Low-cost funds build greater wealth over time.
4. Low-cost funds can be less volatile because they reflect whole sectors of the market.
5. Low-cost funds offer better diversification.
6. You know what you are paying for. No high-salary managers.
7. Low-cost funds don't require you to hope the manager will predict the future correctly. The odds of doing it are 1 in 15,000 each year separately. Over time, all funds provide average returns minus their costs.
8. Low-cost funds are easy to buy.

> "Professional money management is a gigantic **rip-off**."
> Bill Gross, star bond manager,
> *Everything You've Heard About Investing is Wrong*

Summary of many studies about index investing

First, fund managers try to predict the future of the market when they buy and sell securities in their funds. There is no proof this can be done well over time. Yesterday's winners are usually tomorrow's losers. The AVERAGE market return has been 10-12%, so a few managers will beat the average by luck—Just not the same ones every year. nytimes.com/2008/07/13/business/13stra.html **Second**, the costs of the manager, their staff and operations must be paid for by you whether or not they earn you a dime. It is always better to pay as little as possible for the same performance. Costs can take 63% of our returns over time. Surprisingly, while the stock index rose 11.11%, investors with high paid managers averaged only **3.69%** annually for 30 years ended 2013. DALBAR's annual QAIB

Third, high cost managers get paid for increasing the size of their funds, not for making you rich. Bringing in more money is a full-time job. It is expensive to market the funds given that there are now thousands available. It is inevitable that popular funds will grow until they produce average returns with high expenses. Managers want to be rich, not right.

Fourth, there is much less chance of you being treated poorly by fund management if the structure and governance are customer-oriented like Vanguard's and TIAA-CREF's are.

Fifth, many professional managers, pension funds, and Wall Street insiders place their core assets in low-cost index funds.

The **best predictor** of the success of a mutual fund is its cost. Why pay more than you have to? Usually the least expensive funds that match market averages beat the more expensive managed funds. Low-cost market index funds buy all the securities represented in a broad market. The goal of an index fund is to match its market. Low-cost index funds have provided returns that beat 80-90% of managed funds over the long-term. No manager has been able to predict the future so the returns regress to the mean—the 10%-12% average. Wealthy people bet on the averages not the long shot. They don't like to lose value. The patient investor is rewarded in the long run. We grow rich using the simple strategy of riding the whole market at low cost in a tax-FREE account.

> "**In every single time period and data point tested, low-cost funds beat high-cost funds**."

6

Buy groups of stocks of growing companies

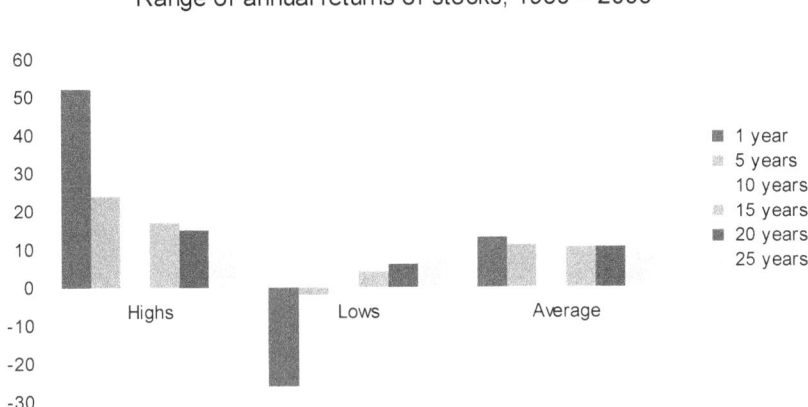

Range of annual returns of stocks, 1950 – 2000

If we want to have $1,000,000 for tax-FREE income, we need a way to make it happen—a strategy. To be able to have a nest egg of $1 million requires that we know how and where to invest, invest regularly, invest properly, monitor accumulations along the way, and get help when we need it. We need a clear plan that takes only one hour to set up and only one hour per year to manage. Complicated plans just don't work for most people. Complicated strategies cost more to execute.

Picking *individual* stocks as a strategy is NOT likely to work for us. Professional managers and day traders have had limited success **over time**, unless they have insider information. Our strategy is to build wealth as a **silent partner** in growing global companies. Since it is unlikely that we (or anyone else) will be able to pick the next 'Apple,' we must invest in a large group of firms. We do not need to fear picking the wrong one or picking one at the wrong time. As the founder of the largest mutual fund firm, John

Bogle, says: "Don't look for the needle. Buy the haystack."

This is contrary to the myth of Wall Street 'professionals.' They make their living claiming to find the needle every year and we pay the price. Professionals promise that they can find the next big one and we pay them well because we want to be rich. But....

Like the lottery, we kid ourselves into thinking that "someone has to win, why not me." We don't believe we are wasting our money even though our rational mind knows that our chance of winning is low. Managed funds don't beat the market most of the time. The odds are like those of a lottery—18 million to 1. Like the lottery, when we invest in a managed fund to "beat the market" we don't count up the costs of all the "tickets." We may buy $25 worth of tickets a week and end up winning $1,000 in a year. We spent $1,200 for $1,000.

In the same manner, a mutual fund manager advertises that their fund has "beaten" the market and so we pay 1-3% of our assets every year. Over time we find that while the stock market index rose over 11% a year during the last 30 years, we earned less than 4%. This is what happened to retail investors according to Dalbar's QAIB recent study.

Some of us keep switching to the 'hot' funds according to the advertising we see. Some are always chasing the last successful mutual fund. Some buy the fund at the high point because they want the winner. They sell the fund when it falls and they want the next high flier. Over time they never earn the return promised by the manager. Past advisor success is no predictor.

In this way, activity can take up to 63% of their returns over time. Each time they sell and buy, they give up earnings and perhaps part of their money if they use a sales person charging 4%. Even if they stay with one managed mutual fund that has annual fees of 1-3%, they are killing the miracle of compounding.

Using the compounding calculator, we can see that our accumulation drops to $0.7 million if we earn 10% instead of 12% annually. We could have $1 million in about 26 years at 11.5% using low-cost funds, no tax and no trading. http://www.moneychimp.com/calculator/compound_interest_calculator.htm

Another Wall Street myth is that investing in market index funds will produce **only** average (mediocre) returns. It is true that the returns will be close to the returns of the market. However, historically the market returns are the ones that are somewhat predictable. Investing in companies inside an index provides no guaranteed return but the average returns have held steady since the 1930s when they started keeping records.

Wall Street's history is littered with strategies that were said to beat the market. The brilliant stock pickers have also come and gone (to the bank). Today, though, which one still working are we going to invest with? Forget the BS. The ONLY thing we really know is that the averages of broad market indexes have produced 10-12% on average each year. See page 32.

For example, some of clients use these Vanguard mutual funds which have earned over 11% for a long time. Of course, there is no guarantee of future returns, but they have all done fairly well. Most started with the 500 Index and added companies in the Energy, Health and International sectors. These 10 funds have done well over time. Many investors pick Vanguard funds because the funds are well run at cost. No "bells and whistles." No expensive CEOs, managers or marketing BS. No owner or broker taking profits from our investment returns, even when there are none.

2013 Total Return	Fund	Long-term Return*	Longevity
32.3%	500 Index	11.0%*	since 1976
18.4%	Energy	13.2%	since 1984
38.4%	Extended Market Idx	11.2%	since 1987
43.2%	Health	17.1%	since 1984
23.0%	International Growth	11.2%	since 1981
39.7%	PRIMECAP	13.7%	since 1984
37.6%	Small Cap Index	10.9%	since 1960
9.2%	Wellesley Income	10.1%	since 1970
36.1%	Windsor	11.6%	since 1958
30.7%	Windsor II	11.1%	since 1985
30.9%	Average	12.1%	

*Average Annual Returns as of 12/31/13.

My clients are patient long-term investors, not speculators. They believe that investments in low-cost funds (index and team-managed) are their best chance of reaching their goals. They have been rewarded for that belief. Vanguard has many low-cost funds and their customer service is better than most funds provide.

Remember, we are buying firms for the long-term. Most

pension funds are invested in stock and bond indexes. Even though the market fell 39% in 2008 and jumped 32% in 2013, the average was still holding. Average returns mean we do not suffer the lowest lows nor the highest highs. Returns 'regress' to the mean: 10-12%.

Most of the largest growing companies in the world are held by these funds. Large US firms are now earning at least **half of their profits overseas** so we are benefiting from growth around the world. This is important because we don't want to miss important earnings progress as the developing nations like China and India expand their economies.

We don't know exactly which companies will be winners so we participate in all of them. We want to own some smaller growing companies too. If they become successful, they will move to the large company funds. We are exposed to almost all areas of the global economy by buying shares of these mutual funds at the lowest cost. We suffer the ups and downs of the markets just like every investor. However, we see that some funds do better at certain times while others do worse. Together we see clients hitting their goal of 10-12% average annual returns.

This type of investing has the greatest chance of avoiding severe swings in the balance of our accumulation. This type of strategy—investing in different types and sizes of companies in different sectors around the world—is called Modern Portfolio Theory. It is probably the best way to assure you of predictable retirement income too.

Modern Portfolio Theory

Some clients use the MPT strategy to control risk while increasing returns. MPT (Moneychimp.com/articles/risk/riskintro.htm) holds that if we put our eggs in different baskets of assets that grow at different times, then the value of all our 'eggs' grows with fewer ups and downs. We can manage the ups and downs of equity funds by buying different ones over time. Higher risk assets are small caps, REITs and foreign stocks. This strategy earns 10-12% with 30% less volatility.

Members assemble asset classes (see http://www.callan.com/research/download/?file=periodic%2ffree%2f757.pdf) that fit their risk-reward tastes. According to this Nobel Prize-winning strategy moneychimp.com/articles/risk/portfolio.htm, a high return asset with a low correlation to other assets in the portfolio can actually reduce the volatility of the whole. It may be possible to earn high returns with less risk **overall** as each asset goes up and down at different times. See the example at fool.com/personal-finance/retirement/2007/03/06/5-steps-to-salvage-your-retirement.aspx.

The past provides only PROBABLE futures. But isn't $1,000,000 (plus or minus $100,000) better than $150,000. Your $250/$500-per-month deposit in the bank for about 26 years will be worth about $168,000 after tax compared with about $1 million from stock investing with low fees. Every investor would be better off with $1 million (+/- $100,000) than $168,000 from a bank.

When clients begin investing, they cannot buy all 10 Vanguard funds at once with $500 (couple) per month. Vanguard has minimums on all funds so they can keep their expenses low for everyone. They start with $1,000 in the STAR or target 2060 fund.

There are two ways to start our account.
The easiest way is to save $500 a month in our savings account until we have the $1,000 minimum for Vanguard's entry fund: STAR #56. We can open the Roth IRA by phone or online: STAR minimum is $1,000. Most Vanguard funds need $3,000 to start. We can keep contributing to this index fund until we have $3,000 for the 500 Index and then $3,000 for the Extended Market funds. Vanguard is at 800.551.8631. STAR has returned 9.9% since 1985.

The second way to begin is to open a Roth IRA at TIAA-CREF, the world's largest pension company, primarily for educational and research institutions. Low expenses and low initial contributions make TIAA-CREF an organization we can stay with for life. TIAA-CREF 800.842.2888.

At TIAA-CREF.org, we can make application and begin immediately with an automatic monthly contribution of $100 or more from our bank account. We can follow how the assets grow by themselves. TIAA-CREF has two funds that provide us with the diversity of companies worldwide: TIAA-CREF Equity Index and TIAA International Equity.

Request a *prospectus* (owner's manual) for each fund you will be using at Vanguard or TIAA-CREF. Both mutual fund firms have experienced salaried representatives that provide accurate information about accounts and funds. Both offer low-cost index funds that hold a broad representation of the market returns of 10-

12%. This is a building block to accumulating wealth.

Both firms are focused on <u>you</u>, not on profits.

This simple strategy provides long-term returns of 10-12% annually on average with the benefit of avoiding single company or industry failures. It provides exposure to new growth potential around the world with less risk than holding one company, one sector, or one country. ***Ten funds provide income, growth and diversification for the rest of your life.***

7

Spend less than you earn

Cost matters!
10-year returns, all equity funds

*Source: Morningstar avg. ann. returns for 10 yrs ended 8/03.

We need to find at least $250 per month to invest in order to build Wealth. We can build wealth by following the strategy outlined in the previous chapters, but we need to have at least $250 available in the first place. In my experience, it doesn't matter how much people earn, most say they don't have the $250 a month to invest for their future. "Today is hard enough," they complain.

Yes, that may well be, but if we don't find the $250-$500 we won't be content tomorrow. We have to go back to our goal. We want to build wealth: accumulating $1,000,000 over time. Based on the way wealth compounds, we need to identify at least $250 a month on a permanent basis. We need to invest consistently or the miracle of compounding will not work.

No one wants to be restricted in their spending. And yet most people want to be content with their life. We must begin where we are. I have found that most people don't mind saving $250 a month on expenses they don't need to make. In fact, they become proud of finding the wasted money.

If we consciously spend our income on those items on our priority list, we can't fail to develop the savings habit. We are teaching ourselves that we can have whatever we want, in time. We are not saying "no" to our desires. We are saying that all we want is on our list and we are working on our list. We will get what we want eventually.

Our future is part of our immediate needs in the sense that if we don't prepare now, we won't have the future we want. Accumulating a $1,000,000 tax-FREE account is a lifelong process. It is like building a business: it takes patience. We follow the simple steps I explained above.

There are a number of ways to identify the $500 a month we need to build our future. Some clients include the $500 in their automatic bill payment or have the trustee debit their account automatically. The contribution is just another bill like rent, mortgage, utilities, car payment, cable, phone, etc. They live on the balance of their income.

Others set up family goals and decide to put a certain amount in a separate account for each goal. In this way, they keep the wealth building process in the forefront of their monthly bill payments ritual. Others make investing automatic—out of sight.

Whatever way works for you. The important part is changing the status of wealth-building from a vague future to a monthly priority. Making it automatic assures you that you will succeed.

Most clients find that the easiest way is to set up an automatic debit of their checking account by the trustee at the time of the application for the Roth IRA. If we are using a Roth 401k or other employer account, we set up the retirement account with automatic contributions.

The Spending Plan agreement works for all types of goals: college fund, emergency fund, vacation fund, new car fund, business start-up fund, whatever we decide to put at the top of our list of priorities. If we don't have this list, we can make one easily.

Clients who are successful have made written plans in some form or other. They have some idea of how much they will need at some time in the future. For short-term goals we can use our savings account but for long-term (5+ years) goals we need to use higher return mutual funds. Many clients have trouble deciding which investment to use for each goal.

I explained the chart we displayed on page 12 above. Stock mutual funds are the investment of choice for any long-term accumulation goal. As per the chart, annual returns of 10-12% are the norm for any accumulation over 5 years. Once we build up a sizable balance in a long-term account, we can "borrow" from ourselves for short-term needs as long as we pay ourselves back.

Thus, clients have used their long-term accumulation account for vacations, cars, appliances, emergencies, etc. This works if they pay themselves back. The account is set up as a Roth IRA so the *contributions* are not taxed when used before age 59.5. After that age, there are no taxes at all—NEVER. However, to meet our long-term goals, we have to pay ourselves back quickly to take advantage of compounding.

Another benefit of using a Spending Plan is that we become focused on how we spend our money. We are more inclined to buy only what we need. For most of us, when we shop for groceries, we seek to get the most for our money by shopping for discounts and by buying in bulk. In the last ten years, the financial services industry has started to offer better values on products. We can avoid overpaying the middle people and buying products we really don't need. We can buy direct, without the middle person.

How can we buy direct? The *Insiders Guides* provide an easy way to save $3,000 or more on financial products we already use. There are buyer's Guides for each specific area. We review some of the ways to find $250 in savings in the next chapter.

We *can't* build wealth by spending more than we earn. Building wealth takes patience and commitment to investing every month. Our wealth-building strategy is about simplicity and patience. We let the trustee debit the $250-$500 every month so we can't fail to create our tax-FREE $1,000,000.

Are you paying too much?

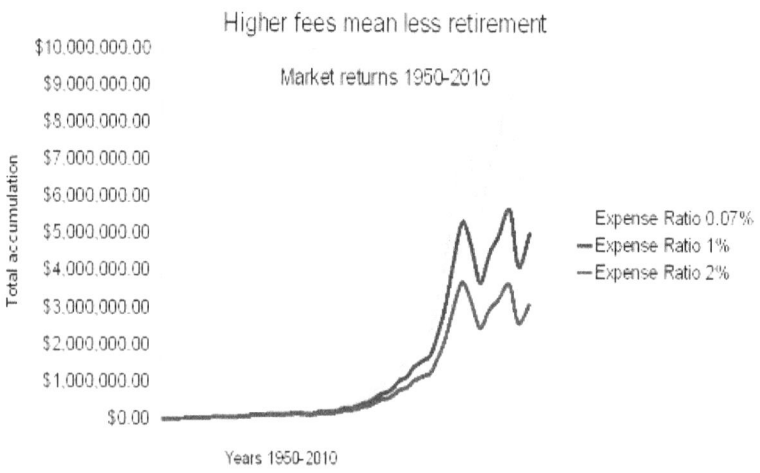

8

Buy only the services you need

Example:

MetLife charged $983 for a $300,000 30-year **term policy**. This same $300,000 benefit was sold by Savings Bank Life Insurance for $384 a year. Their financial strength ratings are A+ and their underwriting requirements are the same. The difference, $599, over 30 years is $17,970. If invested, this difference can add $175,000 to OUR **account**.

It is easy to build wealth if we already have a pile of money. It takes 7-9 years to accumulate $1 million if we already have $500,000. But how do we capture that first $500,000, that $250,000, or even that first $50,000? It comes from buying assets that 'grow by themselves.' It takes time and the easiest way to make sure we reach our goal is to make our monthly contributions automatic like a mortgage payment from our bill pay bank.

But where do we get the $250 or more? The best way is to "REDIRECT" the **cash we already spend** on things we really don't need or can buy for less. This can be your future:

While working with clients, I have found that most of us waste $3,000 or more each year on financial services. We can stop paying for services we don't need. This takes a little thought and questioning on our part, but in reality it is the same process as buying any commodity. When we buy groceries, do we buy the house brand or the one on sale or the one we see advertised? On a little bigger scale, do we buy the new car advertised with a new "push" starter as opposed to a used car with a key? Do we pay an extra $1000 to buy the one with a PC screen to tell us where to go or just use a map? The difference between paying full price for a new car and a 3-year-old model with fewer gadgets can be 40% or more. When we put our future on top of our priority list, we can

REDIRECT the savings to a more worthwhile purpose.

It is the same with financial services. Most of us are not used to shopping for insurance, mutual funds, banking and mortgages. So we don't. We are operating under the mythology of Wall Street —'professionals' say we need them to help guide us, for a price. **But we don't need them anymore**. The world has changed.

Let's take some examples of <u>annual savings</u>:

Auto insurance: save $400 or more EVERY year by changing/dropping some extras we don't need.

Home insurance: save $200 or more EVERY year by changing one limit.

Life insurance: save $1,000 or more EVERY year by using direct to consumer insurer and low-cost term.

Mutual funds: save $2-3,000 EVERY year by using a low-cost provider.

Banking: save $120 EVERY year by using a low-cost provider of the benefits we usually use.

Mortgage: save $2,000 on closings and lower interest rates.

Investments: earn 15-30% guaranteed just by paying off credit cards too.

Tax refund: average $3,052 can pay for $1 million retirement.

Using the Insiders' Guides I put together *The Insiders' Guides to Buying Discount Financial Services: Buy Direct and Save $3,000 Every Year,* we can REDIRECT the $250 a month without having to give up anything important. We don't need to 'tighten our belts' or make a budget. We can give up things we would not benefit from anyway.

I give you a number of testimonials from people who have told about their experience using the Guides.

George B. New York:
"I saved $1,356 on my vehicle insurance using your Insider's Guide to Vehicle Insurance. I saved by using some of your Insiders' 'tricks of the trade' like dropping the extras that I already had."

John D. New York:
"I canceled my life insurance and used the money to buy the mutual funds. You were right. I didn't need the insurance anymore. My kids are all grown. My new wife and I invest as much as we

can now. Your Guide to 'Living' Insurance is a great way to look at our insurance needs."

Mark K. Ohio:

"I had no idea how to invest in the 401k that my new job offered. I have not been disappointed with the mutual funds suggested by other members. I saved about a $1,000 by transferring my old 401k mutual funds to the low-cost funds in your Guide. When I sold my primary residence in 2004, I followed members' advice with the gains. I use all your Guides to help me save more for my retirement since I got a late start. Thanks."

Remember my MetLife example above. I said that people usually pick name brands instead of shopping for services they need. Companies spend a lot for TV advertising and gimmicks that cost you.

Most people are amazed at the difference a little research and shopping can accomplish. Even if we did not have my *Guides*, a search of the Internet would reveal several portals that quote rates. Unfortunately, most people don't take the time to shop or don't know exactly what they need. The Guides help us make the decision of where to shop and what to buy.

Buying only what we need in every financial service area will provide the cash for contributions to our wealth. Taking the time to shop in each area of our expenses helps us make our future happen. Shopping for an hour can add $175,000 to our account. Yes, it is worth it!

The bright future starts with every $250 a month invested. We can spend $30,000 for each $3,000 we invest a year.

Monthly Accumulation at 12% per year									
	5	10	15	20	25	30	35	40	45	50
$100	$8,167	$23,004	$49,958	$98,925	$187,884	$349,496	$643,095	$1,176,477	$2,145,469	$3,905,834
$200	$16,334	$46,008	$99,916	$197,850	$375,768	$698,992	$1,286,190	$2,352,954	$4,290,938	$7,811,668
$300	$24,501	$69,012	$149,874	$296,775	$563,652	$1,048,488	$1,929,285	$3,529,431	$6,436,408	$11,717,502
$500	$40,835	$115,020	$249,790	$494,625	$939,420	$1,747,480	$3,215,475	$5,882,385	$10,727,346	$19,529,169

The Roth IRA Rules

Contributions:

$5,500 ($6,500 over age 50) each year
Income under $131,000 (2016) single
married $193,000 (2016)

Distributions:

Tax-FREE for contributions.
And Tax-FREE for earnings if
Over age 591/2,
Account open 5 years,
Taxable earnings unless
Disabled,
First home ($10,000),
Death

Bonus:

Account can grow tax-FREE for life
Distribution at age 70.5 not required
Heirs don't pay income tax
Account has no maximum

Check with your tax preparer
https://www.irs.gov/pub/irs-pdf/p590a.pdf

9

Manage the account only once a year

We continue to make more money when **_snoring_** than when active.

This is the advice of the most successful investor of our day. He is making it clear that we should NOT touch our investments very often. Contrary to the advice of the Wall Street 'professionals,' he leaves his assets alone to compound over time. He does not follow the 'hot' investment of the day. He buys the stock of growing companies around the world. He has held some investments for over 40 years—Coke, GEICO, AmEx, WellsFargo.

Our emotions tell us to sell when our account balance goes down. We want to buy the next investment hit to make up for previous losses. This is why we have a hard time following Buffett's advice. However, the emotions that cause us to be bad investors are what we can control—not the stock price of growing companies worldwide. Patience is a habit we can learn.

Our contributions to our account need to be automatic so we **buy more shares when the market is down** and less when it is up. This helps us control our emotions. When the market is down, we need to look at the line graph on page 16. We don't know when the market will be up or down but we see that if we sell, we may

miss the next advance. This is why we have to remember Warren Buffett's advice and hold on to stocks. In fact, Mr Buffett says "**our favorite holding period is forever.**"
http://www.berkshirehathaway.com/letters/1988.html

When we own a broad cross-section of the market, we really **don't have to worry** about buying and selling our mutual funds. There is no better investment for the long term. Besides, what would we buy if we sold? We have seen that stocks are the safest investment for periods over 10 years. Patience is profitable.

We believe that the only way to avoid bad investment decisions is to NOT make any investment decisions in haste. Stick with the idea that we only have to look at our tax-FREE account once a year. At that time, I make sure I am making contributions to the specific mutual fund I need to build in order to keep them equally funded. I don't sell because there is no safer investment.

For instance, when I first started investing, I used the 500 Index. After I had accumulated enough to buy the Extended Market, I sold shares of 500 Index ($3,000) and bought it. I kept investing into the 500 Index until I had the minimum for the next one on the list. I repeated this pattern until I had the minimum in each. Then I picked one to add $250 a month for one year. The next year, I did the same until I completed the list again and again.

Today, I am still making contributions using the same rotation. Once a year, I compare the total account balance to where I think it should be. I note what happened during the year for any one fund. I go to the Vanguard site and read about that fund. Do I need to make a change? No, usually I don't. I use the 10 funds listed above. They have consistently done well over the years.

Notice that when we buy each fund at first, we have to sell shares in the 500 Index to do so. Because we are using a Roth IRA, there is no tax on this sale if the share price has gone up. Also, each year, our dividends are re-invested without paying tax on that income. This is part of the miracle of compounding. Our account is growing without taxes each year. Any other non-retirement account would be diminished by the tax paid each year.

There is no need to sell funds that have done well in order to re-balance the 10 funds' balances equally. Most of the research shows that re-balancing each year does not change the long-term outcome of the whole portfolio. Some clients use their contributions each year to add to the fund that has grown the **least**.

However, as each fund becomes larger, the effect of adding contributions becomes smaller over time. At retirement, we can shift from stock funds to the Wellesley Income fund.

When we have to sell shares to meet an emergency or avoid interest payments by using cash for large ticket items, we may sell shares in each fund by equal dollar amounts. This is a better strategy than selling shares in only one fund since we don't know which fund may recover the fastest going forward. In the same way as accumulating shares, we need to reimburse our account for the amount used. It is very desirable to also continue to make contributions at the regular rate—$250-$500 per month. This way we are assured of catching up to our position as we reach our goal.

However, we found that after accumulating a large proportion of our goal, making contributions did not seem to matter to the outcome. For instance, the client whose account is shown on page 22 took $25,000 for a used luxury car in the year the account hit over half a million. He also stopped making contributions. His account total did not suffer long term.

Actually this client redirected his $250 monthly contribution to his grandchild's Roth IRA so that they might have a financial foundation all their life. If he keeps giving this $3,000 a year to his offspring for 20 years, they could have $1,000,000 by age 50. The grandchild "earns" $3,000 a year doing odd jobs for him. Learn more about this "Gift of a Lifetime" in my book, amazon.com/Give-your-Grandchild-2,000,000-Lifetime/.

Our tax-FREE retirement income account does not require us to hire an advisor to manage it. Advisors do not know what the future holds anymore than we do so paying them 1-3% each year just reduces our annual returns. Their fees/charges can take up to 63% of our total accumulations over time. We are investing for the long term and there is proof that switching from one fund to another during the year only hurts our results. As we add more contributions, we can rotate through each fund. The less we tamper with our fund balances the better our experience will be. Remember, we are silent partners in growing businesses around the world.

This is how we create our **Wealth.** It is easy if we learn patience.

Your 'Action' Plan
This is how to build wealth:

This week:
Goal
Set up Roth IRA and start automatic contributions with trustee

This month:
Goal
Do Nothing with investments; don't watch

Next month:
Goal
Do Nothing with investments; don't listen to market media

This year:
Goals
Check fund totals and redirect automatic contributions if necessary

2nd year:
Goals
Check fund totals and redirect automatic contributions if necessary

3rd year:
Goals
Check fund totals and redirect automatic contributions if necessary

4th year:
Goals
Check fund totals and redirect automatic contributions if necessary

Every year:
Goals
Check fund totals and redirect automatic contributions if necessary

10

Take $80,000 tax-FREE each year in retirement

We have learned how to accumulate $1,000,000 or more the **simple** way. We have been **fortunate** that the historical averages of market returns have produced the accumulations we set as our goals.

NOW WHAT?

Now we can take $80,000 out of the accounts each year and pay no income taxes. As of 2015, most states follow the IRS code on our Roth IRA—§ 408 trust—account. No state tax.
http://www.irs.gov/retirement/article/0,,id=137307,00.html

Some clients have moved some of their accumulations into tax-FREE bond funds in order to provide a monthly income to their checking account. They created a retirement spending plan that assured them of that monthly income of a fixed dollar amount with this Guide. amazon.com/Your-Retirement-Spending-Plan-enough

We have to create our $1,000,000 nest egg in order to provide the same buying power as we have today because of inflation. I am assuming that most families will need at least $40,000 (current dollars) a year to live on in retirement. We don't know what will happen to Social Security by 2033. We don't know what employer pensions might look like by then. I am assuming that inflation will continue at a 3% rate. It might be more or less. I have no idea. However, we must prepare for inflation.

At 3%, inflation will make the goods we now buy for $40,000

cost about $80,000. This is not exact. I don't know what will happen in 30 days let alone 30 years. If Social Security or employer pensions can provide our basic income, that is fine. But we don't want to count on them. We need to grow our accounts.

I am using $40,000 as a basic needs income because that has been my experience of what working people desire. It is also an amount that could be generated for life by our $1,000,000 account balance. Many clients use 7%-8% as a target for their investment returns in retirement. This is just an approximation of the average returns over time. Our Vanguard 10 provide over 10%.

Some clients transfer some of their money into a balanced fund like *Wellesley Income* in order to generate the income for the coming year. The balance of their tax-FREE account remains in the broad market funds we have listed above. These funds may continue to produce returns in the 10-12% range. If there is a bad year like 2008, we are not taking money out of our principal at a bad time. We take the money from the Wellesley Income fund with 60% income-earning bonds with 9-10% total return since 1970.

The funds we have listed above include some of the most consistent low volatility returns over time. The Wellesley Income fund has produced about 10% per year on average since 1970. It contains stocks and bonds. **This fund alone might be our source** of annual withdrawals of interest and dividends. Since our **account** is not taxable, there are no tax considerations in the decision of which fund to tap for our monthly income.

Because we have no tax liability on this income of $6,666.66 per month, we may not have to pay tax on our other income like Social Security and/or our qualified retirement funds. 85% of Social Security benefits are currently subject to federal income taxes. The IRS worksheet determines the percentage based on all our other income. Typically those with little or no other taxable income currently have no tax due on their Social Security benefits. Pensions, 401k, IRAs, and annuities are taxed as earned income since we did not pay tax on the contributions (or most of them).

In most cases, we will pay little income tax on our income in retirement since the bulk of it, $80,000 ($40,000 adjusted for inflation), will be tax-FREE. This will give us 25-30% more cash to spend compared with others who have taxable income. Pensions and other taxable income may be taxed at even higher rates in the future to pay for the two wars and two tax cuts since 2001.

(America has never gone to war and taken tax breaks at the same time before so this will take time to pay off.)

Our tax-FREE income will provide us with most of our needs. If we continue to follow the same strategy, we will find a comfortable lifestyle throughout the 30 to 40 years of not working unless we want to.

I and many clients are assuming we will work at least part time after we take full retirement and begin collecting Social Security. If benefits are cut, we will need to work. We are encouraged to use our tax-FREE income to develop a small business since this can help us control the income that is taxed.

As I mentioned at the beginning of this book, many working millionaires are self-employed. Running a small business is a great way to control the taxes we pay. Taxes are the biggest killer of wealth building. It destroys the compounding factor.

The accumulation of $1,000,000 over time can be achieved with patience and perseverance. Spending the income that $1,000,000 can generate may require us to take some principal from time to time. If we use the same wealth building strategy to do this, we will probably have enough to take care of long-term health care and other unforeseen expenses. Since we don't know what may happen, we will want to continue the same habits we have developed before retirement. We live within our means.

We may find that we will have a sizable legacy as we age. There are many ways to pass on our wealth that don't require attorney fees and complicated legal formulations. Many clients have found that incremental gifts to charity and family provide immediate gratification. They have used the suggestions for wealth transfer I presented in the *Retirement Spending Plan*.
amazon.com/Your-Retirement-Spending-Plan-enough/dp/1461084016/

Our retirement income is tax-FREE and has the purchasing power of about $40,000 in today's dollars. Wealthy people who actually earned it don't go out and buy a mansion and the trappings of the wealthy when they retire. They usually have paid off their homes. They travel and share with family. Some continue to earn income doing what they enjoy or provide help to others in their volunteer efforts. Our nest egg and all the earnings are TAX-FREE. We can spend it!

How to Buy Securities For Retirement

1. Cost matters: Broker/advisor cost 1% to 3%

If you use a salesperson, fees can cost HALF A NEST EGG!
$6,000 per year @11% for 28 years = $1,064,740
$6,000 per year @11-1% for 28 years = $885,795
$6,000 per year @11-2% for 28 years = $738,807
$6,000 per year @11-3% for 28 years = $617,570

2. Broker/advisor stock picking does not beat index funds over the long run. No money manager has been able to beat the market consistently. **No one can forecast the future**.

3. Time is the key to investment success. The chance of you buying AND selling, both, at the right times, is near zero.

4. A Tax-FREE investment account increases your balance 25%.

5. Putting all your money in one stock or market sector guarantees failure over time. No one investment is perfect.

6. 'Dollar cost average' buying technique lowers the cost of shares over time. When you invest a fixed amount each month, you buy more mutual fund shares when the price is low and less when high. Over time, you will own more shares at a lower average cost.

7. If you don't have 28 years, convert part of your 401k or IRA to a Roth IRA each year, paying tax annually. Retirement can last 30!

8. Market down? Look at Tom's account balances again, p. 22.

Get what you pay for: pay less; increase earnings

Fiduciary duty is the standard for all who manage other people's money, except brokers/advisors. It is what accountants, lawyers, pension funds, trust companies, and some money managers do.

Although the new law was canceled, you can still have the BEST deal for you. Investment advice is subject to two conditions: the future is unknown and advisors are biased. No person or computer knows the future. American businesses give the closest thing to a sure thing by providing about 11% per year.

Our fiduciaries, Buffett and Bogle have fewer biases than your broker/advisor. Buffett and Bogle are wealthy and give advice for free to all. Both act as fiduciaries—putting your interests above their own. They know we must prepare for tomorrow by spending less than we earn. They have learned to be patient for their investing 'business' to become successful. Fees and taxes hurt.

We need to **recognize that we don't know everything** about investing. With all his experience, Buffett has learned that NO ONE can beat the collective knowledge and caprice of the market on a regular basis by trading pieces of paper. His advice: don't try. John Bogle is famous for his advice: Forget the needle, buy the haystack. http://www.cbsnews.com/news/john-bogles-10-rules-of-investing/

It is hard to be patient and let our money grow by itself. Most people don't have the experience with a business or stocks of companies they know. They don't see the market the way that Bogle and Buffett do. They see it as a casino where the lucky win or a black hole where they can lose their life savings.

Most of us do not know which businesses will grow quickly in the future. Congress does and wins. We have to "*settle*" for the average returns of 10-12% a year. Each of our $3,000 annual investments would be worth about $30,000 over 20 years in businesses like those in the 10 Vanguard funds above.

Most of us know we will never be able to pick the right companies for the future. Wall Street tempts us by claiming they know. Some of us follow their advice and pay dearly. The industry tells us that *we need **them*** to make money. We pay them $560 billions year after year but only keep 3.79% earnings. Trading stocks does NOT benefit us. pbs.org/moyers/journal/09282007/

A person paying 1-3% of their nest egg every year to an advisor can't then admit they get very little for their money. Most advisors can't beat the return of the market so that $3-5,000 a year in fees is just paying the Wall Street Wolf. Over time the amount we pay rises and can *take up to 63% of our total possible accumulations*. Advisors are biased and like to buy and sell securities creating taxes and commissions that don't help us. Large pensions ***hold*** not trade stocks. businessweek.com/articles/2013-01-24/

The key to reaching our goal of $1,000,000 is compounding of high returns over time. If we pay 2% to earn 10-12%, we net 8-10%. Since we know that no advisor can guarantee 10-12% and most studies show investing directly without a "professional" can yield a better result, there is no reason to give up 2%. Advisors usually charge 1-3% whether they beat the averages or not so it is better to go for the 10-12% on our own. Sales people don't give refunds if they don't beat the market! Avoid their mistakes.

Buffett and Bogle agree: The clear **winning strategy** is to do nothing but buy low-cost funds and let compounding work its miracle. Over time using a tax-FREE account with low costs, we can accumulate enough from $250 a month each at 10-12%. Using a compounding calculator http://www.moneychimp.com/calculator/compound_interest_calculator.htm, we find the range is about 33 years. If each spouse has an account, we can be assured of enough income no matter how long each of us lives.

If we use an advisor, we may give up 63% of our total accumulation. Research has shown that the average investor with an 'advisor' earns 3.79% not 11% over time.

This wealth strategy works because it employs a simple method using a unique **tax-FREE trust account** that eliminates the biggest killer of wealth: TAXES. We have seen that compounding over time is the real engine for building wealth. Most people are NOT going to be successful at this because they are impatient and don't let compounding do the work. Plus they pay high fees which are the 2nd biggest killer of wealth.

We will never be taxed on this money—it is like Uncle Sam "giving" us $300,000! We avoid the 25% Fed and 5-7% tax of most states on income from our $1 million account.

We can be our own masters of tax-FREE income with patience. There is no need to pick individual stocks or hire expensive advisors or product pushers with hidden fees. We can do it ourselves with our simple strategy. All we need to do is start our investment plan and then do … NOTHING.

You must take the first step. I don't have a product to sell you so I won't be calling you. You have to call non-profit Vanguard or TIAA-CREF yourself to set up your account. It takes about an hour to set up a Roth IRA for each of you. You can do it online or by phone. You can begin with TIAA-CREF or Vanguard. They have licensed advisors too. Put the contributions on automatic so you don't have to decide every month whether to invest. That is usually how people fail. Life happens and there is always an emergency that requires cash. But future life happens too and you want to be spending your tax-FREE $80,000 a year; not praying Washington won't cut your Social Security Medicare benefits every year.

There is a clear reason why we become wealthy. It is neither luck nor inheritance. Millions of immigrants to this country have done it before. They lived below their means. They saved and invested in businesses they worked. They did not let temporary cash flow problems stop them from building wealth. They used this same strategy by any name, every day.

As many clients said,

"I never even miss the contributions because I never see them. Then all of a sudden, I see my statement" [has $25,000, $50,000, $250,000, $1,000,000.] "We are talking real money here." ***Set it and forget it.***

Do NOTHING!

Call to set it up then forget it

Call Vanguard 800.551.8631 or TIAA-CREF 800.842.2888 today.
https://investor.vanguard.com/what-we-offer/iras/traditional-iras-and-roth-iras

or

https://www.TIAA-cref.org/public/pdf/mfirains.pdf

NOTES

Priorities   Timeline

Gifts to others   _____

Retirement $1 million   _____

_____   _____

_____   _____

_____   _____

_____   _____

_____

The Author

Ian Sender has been a financial services executive for over 20 years. He was a managing director of sales units of securities firms. He is one of the Insiders who contributed to the *The Insiders Guides* set of buyers' guides edited by Dan Keppel: *The Insiders' Guides to Buying Discount Financial Services: Buy Direct and Save $3,000 Every Year*. Ian lives in New Jersey and the Caymans.

https://www.amazon.com/Insiders-Guides-Discount-Financial-Services/dp/143480593X

Dan Keppel's weekly Alert at http://dankeppel.blogspot.com/ or by email request: www.TheInsidersGuides.com

www.ingramcontent.com/pod-product-compliance
Lightning Source LLC
Chambersburg PA
CBHW071809170526
45167CB00003B/1243